Original title:
Snowfall and Slippers



Author: Alec Davenport
ISBN HARDBACK: 978-9916-94-452-3
ISBN PAPERBACK: 978-9916-94-453-0

## In the Wake of Winter's Breath

The trees stand tall, their branches bare,
Beneath a sky, a muted gray.
Whispers float through the chilly air,
As winter fades, it paves the way.

Soft footprints trace the glistening frost,
Each step a promise, a gentle sign.
The warmth of spring comes, no longer lost,
In this quiet world, a dream divine.

Snowdrops bloom, their petals white,
Bringing life where cold once lay.
Sunbeams dance in morning light,
Chasing shadows of yesterday.

As seasons shift, we learn to trust,
The cycle of life, the ebb and flow.
In winter’s wake, hope stirs from dust,
To greet the warmth that starts to grow.

## Comfort in the Cold

Snowflakes dance in moonlight's glow,
Whispers of warmth in the chilling flow.
Fires crackle with gentle light,
Holding us close on a winter night.

Wrapped in layers, we sip our tea,
Finding solace, just you and me.
The frost may bite, the wind may howl,
Yet here, in our haven, we peacefully prowl.

## Soft Echoes of Winter Nights

Under the stars, the world is still,
Silent moments that time can fill.
Each breath a cloud in the crisp air,
Holding secrets we softly share.

The fireplace crackles, shadows sway,
Dreams and wishes in a tender display.
Outside, the drifts rise like soft sighs,
Painting a canvas beneath the skies.

## Dreams Wrapped in Warmth

Blankets cocoon like a gentle embrace,
Every heartbeat finds its rightful place.
In the stillness, we drift and roam,
Finding comfort in this chilly dome.

Pillows whisper tales of yore,
Of laughter shared and dreams that soar.
With each flicker of the candle's light,
We weave our stories through the night.

## Blanket of Silence

The world outside is hushed and bare,
Snow-laden branches, a vision rare.
Wrapped in a cloak of purest white,
We find our peace in the quiet night.

The stars above begin to gleam,
In this tranquil space, we softly dream.
Resting our heads, we breathe so slow,
In this stillness, we let love grow.

## Lace and Ice

Delicate patterns in frost's embrace,
Nature's own lace, a magical trace.
Whispers of winter in crystalline forms,
Beauty unfolds as the cold weather warms.

Glistening frost on each slender branch,
A dance of the cold in a shimmering trance.
Under the moonlight, the world feels so nice,
Lost in the wonder of lace and of ice.

## Shadows of Silent White

Snowflakes fall softly, wrapped in the night,
Creating a world of shadows in white.
Footsteps are hushed on this delicate ground,
Where whispers of winter are quietly found.

Trees wear a blanket so pure and so still,
Nature's serenity, a tranquil thrill.
In silence we wander, our spirits take flight,
Lost in the magic of shadows of white.

## Around the Hearth's Warm Glow

Flickering flames in a cozy embrace,
Gathered together, we share in this space.
Stories unfold as the embers ignite,
Bonded by warmth in the heart of the night.

Laughter and voices dance in the air,
Together in comfort, without any care.
In the glow of the fire, our worries outgrow,
Home is the haven around the hearth's glow.

## A Blanket of Dreams

Softly we drift on a whispering breeze,
Wrapped in the night, where the heart finds its ease.
Stars twinkle gently, a lullaby's call,
In the expanse where our fantasies sprawl.

Visions and hopes gently weave in the night,
Cradled in dreams where our spirits take flight.
Under the cover of twilight that gleams,
We find our solace in a blanket of dreams.

## Chill's Tender Caress

In the silence of the night,
Whispers of the cold delight.
Breezes weave through trees so bare,
Nature's breath, a tender care.

Snowflakes dance in moonlit grace,
Softly falling, leaving trace.
Underneath the icy skies,
Heartbeats quicken, hopes arise.

## Unraveled Tales on Icy Canvas

Stories etched in frosty air,
Each a secret, bold and rare.
Whispers linger on the breeze,
In the stillness, hearts find ease.

Figures swim in glistening white,
Memories crafted in the light.
With each layer, tales unfold,
Icy dreams both new and old.

**Dreams Drifted on the Wind**

Visions sail on winter's breath,
Carried far, defying death.
Glimmering in the starry glow,
Where only silent whispers go.

Clouds of dreams, both bright and bold,
Spinning stories yet untold.
In the twilight, hopes take flight,
Drifting softly through the night.

## Nightfall in Frosted Slumber

As the day surrenders light,
Hushed beneath the blanket tight.
Stars emerge like distant fire,
Frosted dreams, our hearts inspire.

Silent valleys, soft and deep,
Embrace the world in slumber's keep.
Crystal whispers, shadows blend,
In the night, our worries mend.

## Soft Hues of Chill

The sun dips low, a gentle glow,
Soft hues blend in the evening's flow.
Whispers of frost caress the air,
In twilight's embrace, all seems fair.

Shadows stretch beneath the trees,
A canvas brushed with winter's breeze.
Stars awake in the deepening sky,
As the world wraps in a soft sigh.

## A Dance on Powdered Clouds

Snowflakes twirl in the evening light,
A dance upon clouds, pure and white.
Children laugh, their joy unbound,
As magic carpets of snow abound.

With every step, a crunching sound,
In this winter wonder, joy is found.
Hearts beat fast, in sync with the cold,
As stories of warmth and cheer unfold.

## Cozy Comforts of the Cold

A crackling fire, warmth draws near,
With each soft glow, there's naught to fear.
Blankets wrapped tight, stories shared,
In moments like these, love is declared.

Hot cocoa swirls, a treat divine,
With marshmallow dreams, all hearts entwine.
Outside may freeze, but inside glows,
In cozy nooks, where the heart knows.

## Gentle Flurries Beneath My Feet

As day breaks new, the flurries fall,
A blanket of white, covering all.
Each crunch beneath, a sweet refrain,
Nature's carpet, soft with the grain.

Footprints trace where the wild winds guide,
In this winter's heart, I choose to hide.
The world slows down, a moment so fleet,
In gentle flurries beneath my feet.

## Step by Step Through the Stillness

In the hush of the night, we tread,
Softly where dreams and silence wed.
Each step a whisper, a gentle trace,
Moving forward in this quiet place.

Stars above shine their silver light,
Guiding us through the velvet night.
With every heartbeat, we find our way,
Step by step, we greet the day.

The world around holds its breath tight,
Wrapped in shadows, hidden from sight.
Yet in the stillness, warmth can bloom,
As hearts awaken from the gloom.

Side by side, with hopes in hand,
We navigate this tranquil land.
Through stillness vast, our spirits rise,
Step by step under starlit skies.

## Winter's Gentle Caress

Snowflakes dance on a breath of air,
Softly falling, without a care.
Blankets white cover all that's seen,
In winter's arms, the world is serene.

Branches droop with a frosty crown,
Nature whispers her chilling gown.
Amidst the cold, a warmth we find,
In every heart, a spark defined.

The world transforms, a quiet bliss,
In every flake, a winter kiss.
Together we wander, hearts aglow,
In winter's light, our spirits flow.

As day fades into twilight's grace,
We find comfort in winter's embrace.
With gentle hearts and dreams we share,
We roam freely in winter's care.

## Whispers of Winter's Embrace

Amidst the hush, the whispers play,
Softly urging the sun’s ballet.
Gentle breezes through branches weave,
In winter's arms, we learn to believe.

Every snowflake tells a tale,
Of frosted dreams that softly sail.
In the quiet, magic whispers near,
As winter's breath draws us here.

The stillness holds a tender tune,
A melody beneath the moon.
Together we dance in nature's trance,
In the soft glow of winter's glance.

With every heartbeat, warmth amends,
The chill lingers as daylight ends.
In winter's embrace, we find our place,
Bathed in the hush of nature's grace.

## Frost-kissed Footprints

In the morning light, all aglow,
Footprints marked in the sparkling snow.
Each step a story, a trace of time,
Whispers of journeys, silent rhyme.

The frost-kissed earth beneath our feet,
Bears the imprint of moments sweet.
Along frosty paths, we wander free,
In this winter wonder, you and me.

The air is crisp, a breath so bright,
Chasing shadows of fading light.
Every crunch is a note in our song,
As we walk through where we belong.

With laughter bright, we fill the day,
In frosted realms where hearts sway.
Together we leave our footprints bold,
In the story of winter, forever told.

## Frosted Paths in Twilight

The sun dips low behind the trees,
Shadows stretch with the evening breeze.
Silvery frost begins to creep,
Covering earth in a hush so deep.

Footsteps crunch on a sparkling trail,
Whispers of night begin to unveil.
Beneath the glow of stars up high,
Frosted paths where dreams comply.

Moonlight dances on icy leaves,
Nature sighs as twilight weaves.
A tranquil charm in the silent night,
Frosted paths in gentle light.

In this moment, time stands still,
Wrapped in peace, the heart can fill.
Every breath a sigh of grace,
Frosted paths, a sacred space.

## The Secret of Winter's Cradle

In a world wrapped in icy embrace,
Winter's cradle holds a secret place.
Flakes like whispers, soft and white,
Blanket the earth in silent night.

Underneath the blanket so pure,
Life stirs gently, quiet and sure.
The secret lies in the heart of snow,
Where dreams are sown and hopes can grow.

Branches glisten with frosty lace,
Nature bows with a tranquil grace.
A lullaby sung by the cold night air,
The secret of winter, tender and rare.

When spring arrives, all will wake,
But for now, stillness is at stake.
In winter's cradle, hopes abide,
A season's secret, warm inside.

## Slumbering Streets in White

Beneath a quilt of purest snow,
Slumbering streets with a quiet glow.
Lanterns flicker, casting light,
On dreams that twinkle through the night.

Footprints vanish, erased by time,
Echoes linger, soft as rhyme.
In the stillness, shadows play,
As daylight slowly fades away.

Children's laughter weaves through air,
A tapestry of joy and care.
Slumbering streets, where secrets sleep,
Wrapped in wonders, once so deep.

With every flake, the world transforms,
In winter's arms, the heart warms.
A moment cherished, frozen tight,
In slumbering streets of glowing white.

## Echoes of a Frozen Breeze

In the hush of the winter night,
Echoes dance in the pale moonlight.
A frozen breeze whispers low,
Tales of magic, long ago.

Each breath a story, soft and sweet,
Carries memories in its retreat.
Snowflakes twirl like dreams in flight,
Filling the world with pure delight.

Stillness reigns in the starry dome,
Nature's heart is far from home.
Yet in the chill, love's warmth resides,
Echoes of winter where hope abides.

As dawn approaches, colors bloom,
Waking life from its frosted tomb.
But in our hearts, we'll always keep,
Echoes of a frozen breeze, deep.

## Winter's Whisper

Snowflakes fall with grace,
Whispering through the trees,
A blanket soft and white,
Embracing all of these.

Frosted windows gleam bright,
As the cold winds do sing,
The nights are calm and clear,
Winter's gentle, sweet sting.

Footprints fade in the snow,
Memories caught in time,
Each breath forms a small cloud,
As silence starts to chime.

Nature holds its breath tight,
In this moment, so still,
Winter’s whisper, soft light,
Fills the heart with a thrill.

## Frosted Dreams

In the stillness of night,
Glistening dreams take flight,
Frosted edges of hope,
Twinkling like stars in sight.

Blankets of shimmering white,
Cover the world with grace,
Wrapped in the arms of cold,
In this enchanting place.

Children play, laughter rings,
Snowmen stand tall and proud,
In fields of frosted dreams,
Joy echoes through the crowd.

As the sun starts to rise,
Painting skies in soft hues,
Frosted dreams softly fade,
Yet leave behind warm views.

## Chilling Embrace

The air is crisp and pure,
Wrapped in a chilling embrace,
Nature's wonder unfolds,
All dressed in white's lace.

Trees adorned with glitter,
Branches bow down with weight,
Whispers dance in the breeze,
Winter's song feels so great.

The world slows to a crawl,
Underneath the soft skies,
As silence blankets all,
We find peace in goodbyes.

With every frosty breeze,
Comes a warmth of the heart,
In this chilling embrace,
Winter plays its sweet part.

## Silent Steps in White

Silent steps through the snow,
Footprints disappear in time,
Each crunch underfoot sounds,
A rhythm, a soft rhyme.

The world wears a white coat,
Sparkling in winter's glow,
While whispers of the cold,
Gently twirl as they flow.

Underneath the pale moon,
A magic fills the air,
Silent steps lead us home,
To warmth beyond compare.

Snowflakes continue to fall,
A dance of pure delight,
In this hush of the night,
We walk on, spirits bright.

## The Color of Winter's Breath

Whispers of frost touch the pines,
Glimmers of white in shimmering lines.
Frozen rivers, shadows of gray,
Winter's breath softly holds sway.

Moonlight dances on fields of snow,
A canvas where quiet dreams flow.
Colors muted, a tranquil sight,
Painting the world in soft white light.

## Paths Woven in Icicle Dreams

Footsteps crunch on the frozen ground,
As nature's magic weaves around.
Icicles hang with graceful ease,
Glistening treasures caught in the breeze.

Down hidden paths where silence grows,
The secrets of winter gently flows.
Each step a story, each breath a thread,
Woven in dreams where the chill is spread.

## A Serenade of the Soft White

Snowflakes drift in a soft ballet,
A serenade to end the day.
Each flake a note, a silken sound,
Falling gently on winter's ground.

The air is crisp, the evening still,
Nature's beauty does quietly thrill.
In the soft glow of the moon's soft light,
Whispers of winter fill the night.

## Draped in Winter's Shawl

Beneath the sky where stars glimmer bright,
Winter drapes a shawl of white.
Each bough adorned with delicate lace,
Nature's beauty finds its place.

Quiet moments wrapped in chill,
A peaceful hush on the world at will.
In the stillness, dreams take flight,
Draped in warmth 'neath the cold night.

## A Tapestry Woven in Frost

Frosty tendrils lace the trees,
Glistening in the morning light.
Nature's canvas, chill and ease,
A quiet beauty, pure and bright.

Icicles hang like crystal blades,
Guardians of the winter's breath.
In their shimmer, daylight fades,
Whispering softly, life and death.

A tapestry of silvery white,
Each pattern tells a tale untold.
In this stillness, shadows bite,
While warmth and solace lie unfold.

Underneath the quilt of snow,
Dreams are cradled, hushed and deep.
Through winter's grasp, the earth will grow,
Awakening soon from her sleep.

## Warmth Nestled within Cold

In the heart of winter’s chill,
Embers glow in hearths aglow.
Wrapped in flannel, time stands still,
Outside whispers frost and snow.

Tea and laughter fill the air,
Footprints trace where joy has been.
In these moments, love we share,
Against the cold, our hearts begin.

Stars blink bright in velvet night,
While shadows dance on frosted panes.
Winter's chill will not ignite,
The warmth that in our spirits reigns.

Through icy winds, our fires burn,
Together facing cold with cheer.
In this season, hearts return,
To find the warmth that draws us near.

## The Spirit of Winter's Lullaby

Snowflakes fall like whispered dreams,
In the hush of twilight's breath.
Nature hums in soothing themes,
Cradling life in quiet depths.

Softly swaying, trees abide,
Wrapped in blankets white and still.
The spirit sings, a gentle guide,
Instilling peace, a tender thrill.

As the night begins to fall,
Stars peek through the shimm'ring veil.
Winter's song, a soothing call,
Guiding us with every trail.

Close your eyes, embrace the night,
Feel the spirit's calm embrace.
Winter whispers, pure delight,
In her arms, we find our place.

## Twilight's Gentle Blanket

Twilight drapes the world in gray,
A blanket soft, so hush and calm.
The sun dips low, ends the day,
Embraced in evening's soothing balm.

Shadows stretch and dance at play,
As stars begin their twinkling run.
Night enfolds the fading ray,
Whispering secrets of the sun.

In this calm, the cold does creep,
Yet warmth ignites within the heart.
As stillness wraps us, dreamers sleep,
In twilight's glow, we play our part.

The world transformed, a fleeting grace,
In this moment, time stands still.
Together here, we find our place,
Wrapped in twilight's gentle thrill.

## Winter's Lull

Snowflakes drift and dance,
As the cold winds softly sigh,
Nature wraps the world in trance,
Underneath the silver sky.

Whispers of the quiet night,
Moonlight bathes the fields in peace,
Every shadow feels so light,
In this stillness, all hearts cease.

Trees adorned with crystal lace,
Glisten in the pale moonbeam,
Time takes on a slower pace,
In this warmth, we softly dream.

Fires crackle, embers glow,
Hot cocoa in our gentle hands,
Winter's lull, the world in snow,
Together here, our love expands.

## Wrapped in Warmth

By the hearth, we share a smile,
Blankets wrap us, close and tight,
With your touch, I feel the while,
Wrapped in warmth, the world feels right.

Outside, the frost begins to bite,
Inside, our hearts are all aglow,
In this cozy firelight,
Time, like falling snow, moves slow.

Laughter dances, fills the room,
As stories weave through winter's air,
With every cheer that starts to bloom,
Wrapped in warmth, we lose our care.

With your laughter, joy takes flight,
In our haven, we find bliss,
Holding close, all feels so bright,
Wrapped in warmth, it’s you I miss.

**Secrets of the Icicle Realm**

Beneath the eaves, they hang so clear,
Icicles like crystals bright,
Holding secrets, whispers near,
In the shimmering, frozen light.

Winter’s breath, a mystic song,
Icicles gleam with tales untold,
In their shadows, dreams belong,
Guarding wonders of the cold.

Nature's art in frosted grace,
Each one forms a story new,
In their depths, we find our place,
Secrets shared, just me and you.

As they melt, the truth reveals,
Glistening drops of time unfold,
In the warmth, our love appeals,
Secrets of the icicle hold.

## Where Dreams Meet Frost

In the hush of winter's chill,
Where dreams and frost begin to blend,
Every flake a whispered thrill,
As the night begins to bend.

Stars are dancing in the skies,
Lit like gems upon the snow,
In the quiet, old heart sighs,
Where dreams meet frost, time moves slow.

Wrapped in layers, soft and warm,
Each breath fogs the icy air,
In this realm, we find our charm,
Where dreams meet frost, we lay bare.

Hand in hand, beneath the moon,
With every step, our spirits race,
In this night, we find our tune,
Where dreams meet frost, our hearts embrace.

## The Language of a Still Winter

Snowflakes dance down from the sky,
Blankets of white cover the ground.
Silence whispers soft lullabies,
In the stillness, peace is found.

Frozen branches, bare and stark,
Nature sleeps, a dream so deep.
A hush blankets the world, so dark,
As the earth in slumber keeps.

Frosty air bites at the skin,
Breath creates clouds that float away.
Time seems to pause, a gentle spin,
In winter's arms, we sway.

Stars twinkle in the icy night,
Moonlight glistens on the sheen.
In this moment, pure delight,
Winter's beauty, softly seen.

# Chasing Soft White Whispers

Gentle breezes carry secrets,
Through the trees, they ebb and flow.
Chasing whispers in the crescent,
Softly dancing, to and fro.

Snowflakes swirl, a ballet grand,
They flirt with shadows, just a tease.
Nature's magic, woven and planned,
In this moment, hearts find ease.

Footsteps echo on the bright ground,
As laughter trails behind and glows.
In these whispers, joy is found,
Like winter's breath, it sweetly flows.

On this journey, dreams unfurl,
Chasing magic through the glide.
With every twist, a magic swirl,
In winter's arms, we confide.

## Tread Softly on Glacial Dreams

In frozen realms where shadows play,
Tread softly on the glacial sheen.
Every step a dance, a ballet,
In the stillness, calm and serene.

Echoes of whispers in chilly air,
Murmurs of secrets hidden deep.
Lost in a world stripped of care,
As dreams in ice begin to creep.

Crystalline structures gleam and shine,
Reflecting light in every hue.
Nature paints with hand divine,
Creating magic, pure and true.

In this silence, hearts align,
With every breath, the world feels bright.
Treading softly, souls entwined,
In glacial dreams, we find our light.

## Muffled Footsteps in the Quiet

In the deep hush of winter's night,
Muffled footsteps wander slow.
Every crunch of snow feels right,
In this stillness, spirits grow.

Shadows loom where soft lights glow,
A lantern's glow casts gentle beams.
Through the world, quiet hearts flow,
Carried forth on whispered dreams.

As stars twinkle in endless skies,
The universe holds breath anew.
In silence, a thousand sighs,
Muffled secrets shared by few.

Among the pines, the air is pure,
Winter's beauty wraps snug and tight.
With every step, feel secure,
In the quiet, find your light.

## When Flakes Descend

Whispers of white swirl in the air,
Each flake dances, float without a care.
Soft blankets cover the world so bright,
A hush falls gently, wrapping the night.

Boughs bend low with a silvery weight,
A wonderland opens, it's not too late.
Children's laughter fills the frozen space,
As snowmen rise in a joyful embrace.

Footprints trace paths through the glistening ground,
Every step crunches with a pleasant sound.
Nature takes pause in serene delight,
While winter weaves magic in purest white.

As night descends, stars begin to gleam,
Under the moon, the world starts to dream.
When flakes descend, time seems to stand still,
A moment wrapped tight in winter's goodwill.

## Garlands of Ice

Frosted branches don a crystal crown,
Nature adorned in a shimmering gown.
Icicles hang like jewels from the eaves,
Garlands of ice weave through the trees.

Morning sunlight kisses the frozen scene,
Sparkling diamonds, a glint so keen.
A canvas painted with intricate care,
Every corner holds winter’s flair.

Soft whispers of wind through the silent wood,
Nature reflects in the beauty of good.
The world holds its breath in a chill embrace,
As garlands of ice grace every place.

With every step on the glistening ground,
A magical feeling in the air is found.
In this winter realm, pure and grand,
Garlands of ice create a wonderland.

## Warmth Beneath the Chill

In the heart of winter, warmth does reside,
Beneath layers thick, where secrets hide.
A cozy fire crackles with delight,
Welcoming all from the cold of night.

Fingers wrapped tight 'round a steaming cup,
As snowflakes fall softly, never abrupt.
Laughter rings out in the room's embrace,
Warmth beneath the chill, a sacred space.

Outside, the world glimmers in silence,
Yet here, we thrive in our own brilliance.
Stories unfold by flickering light,
Hearts glow brighter than the winter's night.

As frost paints windows with delicate lace,
Inside, we gather to share and trace.
Memories woven like a soft shawl,
Warmth beneath the chill, welcoming all.

## A Tapestry of Winter Hues

Crimson and gold in a world turned white,
A tapestry woven, day meets night.
Shadows stretch long as the sun dips low,
Winter colors dance in the softening glow.

Emerald firs stand tall and proud,
Draped in snow, they draw a crowd.
While twilight paints across the sky,
A blend of hues, as day waves goodbye.

The stillness holds secrets, waiting to share,
As the cold air whispers tales everywhere.
Soft pastels brush on the horizon's edge,
A tapestry woven, a delicate pledge.

Under starry skies, all colors ignite,
A celebration of beauty in the night.
In this season where dreams do rise,
A tapestry of winter hues lights the skies.

## Chilly Embrace of the Evening

The sun dips low, shadows stretch wide,
A whispering breeze, nature's guide.
Stars start to twinkle, a silent show,
In the chilly embrace, where dreams can flow.

Leaves rustle softly in the night,
Moon casts a glow, oh what a sight.
Laughter and warmth mingle with chill,
As hearts gather close, time seems to still.

Each breath a cloud in the frosty air,
Moments suspended, none seem to care.
Every glance shared, a secret exchanged,
In the chilly embrace, we feel unchained.

Together we wander, beneath the vast sky,
In this serene silence, we let out a sigh.
Wrapped in the magic of darkening hues,
In the evening's embrace, we find our muse.

## Heartbeats Beneath Layers

Under the layers, our heartbeats rise,
A rhythm unseen beneath soft skies.
Each beat a promise, a silent vow,
In the hush of the moment, we live in now.

Wrapped in the warmth of what we conceal,
Tender connections, a deep-rooted seal.
With every whisper, the world fades away,
In the stillness, together we stay.

Fingers entwined, a lifeline so true,
Through storms and shadows, just me and you.
Beneath the layers where secrets reside,
Our hearts are the compass, our souls the guide.

In the softest silence, we dare to dream,
Each shared heartbeat, a radiant stream.
Through all the seasons, together we'll grow,
Beneath the layers, our love will show.

## The Magic of Frosted Light

Morning breaks with a shimmer so bright,
Nature awakes in the magic of light.
Frost on the grasses, diamonds that gleam,
In this quiet moment, we dare to dream.

Sparkling crystals on branches sway,
Dancing to whispers of dawn's ballet.
Every shadow draped in silver delight,
A world transformed in the tenderness of light.

As the sun climbs high, the chill fades away,
Colors emerge, brightening the day.
Yet still we linger, hearts wrapped in awe,
In the magic of frosted, we find our flaw.

Moments captured in a breath of surprise,
Life's gentle beauty seen through our eyes.
With every soft shimmer, our spirits take flight,
Embracing forever in the magic of light.

## Encased in Soft Moments

Quietly nestled in softest embrace,
Time is a treasure, a sacred space.
Whispers of comfort, low lanterns glow,
Encased in soft moments, our hearts start to grow.

Laughter like music, a sweet, gentle tune,
Filling the air as we dance with the moon.
Every glance shared holds a story so deep,
Encased in soft moments, our memories keep.

Fingers entwined, our worries set free,
Wrapped in the solace of you and me.
Together we journey, nowhere to roam,
Encased in soft moments, we’ve found our home.

Seasons may change, yet still we will stay,
In this cocoon where love lights our way.
Through every soft heartbeat, through silence and song,
Encased in soft moments, is where we belong.

## The Dance of Winter Feathers

Snowflakes swirl in the cold night air,
They twirl and spin, a gentle affair.
Each feather glistens, a diamond's grace,
Whispering secrets as they embrace.

Branches bow softly, their burden light,
Moonlight sparkles, a magical sight.
The world holds its breath, thus time stands still,
In this frozen realm, all hearts can fill.

Silvery shadows glide through the trees,
Nature's ballet dances with the breeze.
Winter's hush is a song so sweet,
A melody wrapped in the softest sheet.

As dawn breaks gently on this white stage,
The dance continues, we turn the page.
In the quiet, a world we savor,
Winter's feathers, a craft of favor.

## Cozy Footprints in Frost

Morning light kisses the blanket of white,
Each step we take feels perfectly right.
Footprints lead on with stories untold,
In a winter wonderland, brave and bold.

Wrapped in layers, we wander the scene,
A tapestry woven in crisp and serene.
Laughter echoes as we play and run,
Chasing the warmth of the golden sun.

Trees stand tall in their frosty attire,
Nature's artwork ignites our desire.
Every footprint tells of our joyful race,
In the heart of winter, we find our place.

The day wears on with a gentle embrace,
In cozy footprints, we find our grace.
Together we stroll through the glistening mist,
Happiness found in each frosty tryst.

## Hushed Mornings Under Blankets

Morning breaks softly, a whispering sigh,
Wrapped in the warmth that will never die.
Blankets caress, as the world drifts away,
In cozy cocoon, we choose to stay.

Outside, the chill nips at the air,
But inside our haven, there's nothing to bear.
With cocoa in hand, we watch the sun rise,
In this peaceful refuge, our spirits can fly.

The world outside shimmers with frost's kiss,
But in our retreat, there's nothing amiss.
Under thick covers, dreams gently weave,
In the stillness of dawn, we dare to believe.

As the day awakens, our hearts remain close,
Finding solace in stillness, we cherish the most.
Hushed mornings linger, a quiet unfold,
Wrapped in our secrets, as stories are told.

## Icy Lullabies

Stars twinkle softly in the night sky,
A blanket of ice where dreams drift by.
Lullabies echo through the chilly night,
Cradled in stillness, everything feels right.

The moon sings sweetly to the frozen ground,
In this serene world, peace can be found.
With blankets of frost that shimmer and glow,
The land wears a gown of pure, sparkling snow.

Whispers of winter float through the trees,
Guiding the night on a gentle breeze.
In the heart of darkness, lullabies play,
A tender reminder of love's sweet sway.

Embraced by the frost, we drift and we dream,
In this winter's hold, everything's a gleam.
With each icy note, our worries take flight,
Lulled into slumber, we bask in the night.

## Glistening Trails of Serenity

In dawn's embrace, the world awakes,
Glistening paths where silence breaks.
Each step a whisper, soft and light,
Unity found in morning's sight.

Golden rays on dew-kissed grass,
Every moment, let it last.
Nature's canvas, painted slow,
In trails of peace where flowers grow.

Rustling leaves with secrets kept,
In the calm, our spirits wept.
A journey marked by tranquil glee,
In harmony, we roam so free.

Through the woods, where shadows play,
Guided by the light of day.
In glistening trails, we find our way,
Serenity blooms, come what may.

## Gentle Frost on Soft Soles

Cold breath whispers through the trees,
Gentle frost on autumn's breeze.
Crisp and clear, the world awakes,
Nature sighs as stillness breaks.

Soft soles crunch on icy ground,
Every footfall's magic sound.
Morning's chill, a sweet caress,
In wintry dance, we feel no stress.

Dew like diamonds on the fields,
To the touch, a beauty yields.
Gentle frost, a fleeting grace,
In this moment, find our place.

As daylight warms the chilly air,
This winter's beauty, beyond compare.
On soft soles, we wander slow,
Through the frost, our spirits glow.

## Enchanted by the Flurry

Amidst the dance of swirling snow,
Enchanted hearts begin to grow.
Flurries twirl in playful grace,
Transforming all, a magic place.

Each snowflake whispers soft and clear,
In the chill, we draw near.
Blankets white on earth's embrace,
In winter's arms, find our space.

Laughter echoes through the air,
Joy is found, it's everywhere.
Enchanted by the wintry glow,
In this wonder, we will flow.

As evening falls, the stars ignite,
Shimmering softly, pure and bright.
In the flurry, we lose our way,
But in our hearts, love will stay.

## The Quiet of Falling White

In the hush where voices fade,
The quiet comes, a gentle braid.
Falling white, like feathered dreams,
Whispers soft, or so it seems.

Each flake a story, unique, untold,
In the silence, warmth unfolds.
Embracing stillness, deep and wide,
In winter's glow, we confide.

A world transformed, serene and bright,
The quiet magic of the night.
In snowy blankets, peace alights,
And love surrounds in shining white.

Through the calm, our spirits soar,
In the falling white, we find much more.
The quiet breath of nature’s heart,
In winter’s arms, we never part.

## Frosted Reveries

Whispers of snowflakes dance in the air,
Glistening like diamonds, a magical flair.
Trees wear white cloaks, serene and still,
Nature's soft hush, a moment to thrill.

Crisp breaths of winter, fresh and clean,
Footprints left softly, a fleeting scene.
Dreams swirl in flurries, lost in the night,
Wrapped in the beauty of pure, soft white.

## Cradled in Winter's Cocoon

Gentle silence blankets the ground,
In this still haven, peace can be found.
Snowflakes descend like sighs from above,
Nature holds close what it dearly loves.

Inside the warmth, a hearth's gentle glow,
Fingers wrapped 'round cups, dreams in tow.
Outside, the world wears a mantle of grace,
Cradled in winter's embrace, a soft place.

## Lost in a Whisper of White

In a world where the colors fade fast,
Whispers of white paint memories that last.
Frozen stillness, a moment of grace,
Lost in the stillness, a tranquil space.

Snow-laden branches bow low with pride,
Each flake a secret, where dreams can reside.
In the silence, the heart learns to hear,
The softest of whispers, both fragile and clear.

## The Tread of Gentle Time

Footsteps echo on a path of soft snow,
Time stretches gently, moving slow.
Moments suspended, a sweet icy thrall,
Each second a treasure, inviting us all.

The world unfolds in a silvery hue,
Memories linger, both old and new.
With every soft breath, the seasons shift,
In the tread of time, we find our gift.

## Veils of Ice on Silent Mornings

Veils of ice on silent morn,
The world adorned, a chilly scorn.
Each breath a whisper, soft and light,
Nature's canvas, pure and bright.

Footsteps crunch on frosted ground,
Echoes of peace, a tranquil sound.
Frozen branches, glistening lace,
In this hush, we find our place.

Sunrise paints the sky in hues,
Gold and pink, a vibrant muse.
The chill retreats, warmth draws near,
In stillness found, we banish fear.

Veils of ice begin to melt,
Revealing all that nature felt.
A silent morn, a fleeting spell,
In winter's grip, all is well.

## Dreams Wrapped in Wool

In cozy nooks where shadows play,
Dreams wrapped in wool, they softly sway.
Embers crackle, warmth surrounds,
A world of peace in quiet sounds.

Blankets thick, embrace me tight,
Soft whispers drift into the night.
The fabric of hope, snug and warm,
As memories weave their gentle charm.

Clouds outside, a wintry chill,
Inside, the heart feels softly still.
In dreams we wander, far and free,
Wrapped in the warmth of yarn and glee.

Awake, yet lost in thought's embrace,
The woolen world, a sacred space.
Where visions dance in twilight hues,
And every stitch sparks joy anew.

## Crystalline Memories

Crystalline memories, frozen bright,
Capture moments, pure delight.
Through frosted glass, a quiet view,
Where time stands still, and dreams come true.

Each flake a story, gently spun,
Whispering tales of joy and fun.
In the stillness, we find our past,
Echoes of laughter, shadows cast.

The world adorned in sparkles fair,
With every breath, the frosty air.
Memories glimmer, soft and clear,
In crystalline forms, we hold them dear.

As seasons shift and rivers flow,
These moments linger, gently glow.
In the heart's keep, forever stored,
Crystalline memories, timeless, adored.

## The Unseen Symphony of Winter

The unseen symphony of winter chimes,
In silence plays the softest rhymes.
Each flake a note, a story told,
In harmony, the world unfolds.

Branches bow with the weight they bear,
Gentle whispers fill the air.
A hidden song, a soft embrace,
In winter's arms, we find our grace.

Frozen rivers, a still refrain,
In every droplet, joy and pain.
Nature conducts with patient hand,
A symphony across the land.

As night descends, the stars align,
Each twinkle part of the design.
In winter's chill, our hearts can sing,
To the unseen beauty that dreams bring.

## Silence Wrapped in White

Amidst the snow, a hush descends,
Whispers soft, where silence bends.
Frosted branches, a tranquil sight,
In the stillness, time feels right.

Footprints lead through drifts of grace,
Nature's canvas, a pure embrace.
Breath clouds form in the crisp, clear air,
In this silence, hearts lay bare.

The world sleeps under blankets deep,
Secrets held, in shadows keep.
Each flake falls with a gentle kiss,
In this moment, find your bliss.

As daylight fades, a glow remains,
Evening whispers through the plains.
Wrapped in white, we find our peace,
In the silence, love won't cease.

## Echoes of a Crystal Dawn

Morning breaks with hues so bright,
Golden rays chase off the night.
In the stillness, echoes play,
Welcoming the brand new day.

Birds take flight with joyful songs,
In the breeze where beauty belongs.
Crystal dewdrops on leaves gleam,
Nature whispers a hopeful dream.

Mountains stand in silent pride,
As the sun begins to glide.
Every shadow starts to fade,
In this light, we are remade.

Breathe it in, this fresh new start,
Let it dance within your heart.
Echoes linger, soft and warm,
In the dawn, we find our form.

## The Art of Cozy Retreats

In the corner, a chair awaits,
Soft and snug, it celebrates.
Wrapped in warmth, a blanket tight,
In this space, the world feels right.

Candles flicker, shadows play,
Flicking light to end the day.
A steaming cup, aroma sweet,
Sips of joy where dreams repeat.

Books stacked high with stories told,
Adventures waiting to unfold.
Time slows down, the clock stands still,
In cozy nooks, we find our will.

Whispers share of hopes and fears,
Echoed laughter, dried-up tears.
In this art of snug retreat,
Hearts align, life feels complete.

## Shimmering Veils of Chill

Winter's breath, a frosty bite,
Veils of chill, both soft and light.
Wrapped in layers, warm and neat,
The world shimmers with its treat.

Stars above, a twinkling sight,
Guiding dreams through the cold night.
Every flake, a dance divine,
Nature's gift in pure design.

Paths of white, we wander slow,
Where the whispers of winter flow.
Each step crunches with crisp delight,
In the hush, the heart feels right.

As the moon graces the sky,
We find solace, you and I.
Shimmering veils in the night,
In the chill, all feels bright.

## Homebound in Frosted Retreats

Snow whispers softly, the world in white,
Shadows of branches, a chill in the night.
Candles flicker gently, warmth in the air,
Homebound in dreams, without a single care.

Footsteps crunch loudly, on paths draped in snow,
The world seems enchanted, time moves slow.
Blankets wrapped tightly, outside winter’s song,
Nights cradled by silence, where hearts belong.

## Silver Threads on a White Night

Moonlight cascades on the snow-dressed trees,
Whispers of night carried on the breeze.
Silver threads twinkle, across the vast sky,
Painting the darkness, where dreams softly lie.

Cold winds may blow, yet warmth fills the heart,
A dance of reflections, where shadows depart.
Glistening frost covers the world like lace,
In this charming silence, we find our place.

## The Embrace of Winter's Blanket

Winter’s embrace, a soft lullaby,
Cradled in comfort, as time drifts by.
Each flake is a whisper, from skies up above,
The chill of the air, but the warmth of our love.

Clouds cloak the heavens; stars peek through night,
Every heart kindles a flickering light.
Wrapped in a blanket, we sit side by side,
In the stillness of winter, our hearts open wide.

## Frosted Reflections

Morning dew glimmers on branches of pine,
Frosted reflections in shadows align.
Nature's own canvas, both stark and divine,
Every breath is fragrant, a crisp, pure design.

Gentle the moments, we cherish them true,
Each flake is a secret, each sunset a hue.
Life's fleeting beauty, in silence it gleams,
In frost-kissed whispers, we find all our dreams.

## Starlit Paths of White

Under a sky of shimmering light,
Footsteps dance in the snow so bright.
Guided by stars, we wander free,
A tapestry woven, for you and me.

The chill in the air, so crisp, so clear,
Echoes of laughter we hold so dear.
As dreams take flight on this winter night,
We trace our way on paths of white.

Each flake a whisper, soft and slow,
Kissing the ground where our hopes will grow.
Together we walk, hand in hand we roam,
Finding a place where our hearts call home.

Beneath the glow of the silver moon,
We lose ourselves to the night's sweet tune.
In silence we share our secrets bright,
On starlit paths wrapped in winter's light.

## Embracing the Frozen Quiet

In the hush of the morning, life stands still,
Frosted whispers wake, at the dawn's will.
Blankets of snow cover all we see,
A world paused in tranquil serenity.

Each breath a cloud, frozen in time,
Nature's heartbeat, a soft, gentle chime.
The trees wear coats of shimmering white,
Guardians of secrets, cloaked in the night.

As shadows lengthen, the day drifts away,
Stars gently flicker, bidding goodbye to day.
Embracing the stillness, we find our peace,
In this frozen quiet, our worries cease.

With each passing moment, we linger and sigh,
Lost in the beauty where silence will lie.
In the heart of the winter, we find our return,
Embracing the quiet, where our spirits can burn.

## Whispers on the Wind

The breeze carries secrets from lands afar,
Soft little tales, like a wishing star.
Nature's soft voice calls to us gently,
In the rustling leaves, our hearts can be free.

It dances through branches, weaving its song,
A melody sweet, inviting us along.
We close our eyes and let it sweep,
Taking us places where dreams softly creep.

With every gust, we feel its embrace,
A tender reminder, we find our grace.
Whispers of wonder, touching our skin,
Guiding our thoughts from within to begin.

Each sigh of the wind holds a tale untold,
Mysteries loom in the air, manifold.
And as shadows deepen, the whispers grow clear,
Calling us home, where love draws near.

## Footprints in the Crystal

Wandering softly on a sparkling trail,
Footprints linger in the snow, without fail.
Each step a promise of journeys ahead,
In the hush of the ice, where dreams are bred.

The world wears a coat of shimmering white,
Every corner aglow in the pale moonlight.
Sculpted and pure, the landscape unfolds,
Stories of warmth in the freezing cold.

We chase the horizon, our laughter a song,
In this winter wonderland, we feel we belong.
With every imprint, we write in the frost,
Memories captured, never truly lost.

As evening descends, the footfalls grow faint,
Each moment we cherish, no room for complaint.
In the beauty around us, we find our delight,
Footprints in the crystal, preserved in the night.

## Shadows Walk Softly

In the quiet of the night,
Shadows dance with delight.
Whispered secrets in the air,
Softly tread without a care.

Moonlight glimmers on the ground,
Silent footsteps all around.
Each step a gentle kind of grace,
In this hidden, tranquil space.

Beneath the veil of silken dark,
They leave not a trace, but a spark.
In shadows where dreams awake,
A world of wonder they create.

## Glimmers of Frosted Joy

Frosty mornings greet the sun,
Nature's sparkle, a joyful run.
Every branch a crystal flare,
Whispers of joy fill the air.

Children’s laughter, warm and bright,
Chasing glimmers in the light.
Snowflakes fall like soft, sweet dreams,
Painting wonder, bursting beams.

Frosted echoes of delight,
Filling hearts with purest light.
In each sparkle, stories flow,
Glimmers of joy in winter’s glow.

## The Palette of Frozen Moments

Brush of cold upon the scene,
A palette rich with silver sheen.
Each moment frozen in a hue,
Nature's artwork, fresh and new.

Time stands still, a gentle pause,
Captured beauty, nature's laws.
Colors blend in soft embrace,
The art of winter's quiet grace.

In every flake that we behold,
Stories of warmth, yet untold.
Frozen moments, fleeting bliss,
A canvas kissed by winter's kiss.

## Crystal Thoughts in a Frosty Mind

Thoughts like crystals, pure and clear,
In winter's hush, they draw near.
Shimmering light upon the frost,
In quiet moments, never lost.

Contemplation in the cold,
Layered stories yet unfold.
Each reflection pure and bright,
Guided by the soft moonlight.

Frosty whispers in the breeze,
Notions flutter, hearts at ease.
In the stillness, dreams align,
Crystal thoughts in frosty mind.

## Embracing the Icy Embrace

In the stillness, cold winds blow,
Crystals dance, with a twinkling glow.
Snowflakes whisper, secrets untold,
Nature's canvas, painted in bold.

The world wrapped tight in a frosty shroud,
Silence reigns, peaceful and proud.
Footprints crunch on the frozen ground,
An echo of joy, in silence, found.

Beneath the branches, a soft sigh,
As frost kisses each leaf and spry.
Time stands still in the icy embrace,
A moment of beauty, we fervently chase.

With every breath, a shimmer of light,
Winter's magic, heartwarming and bright.
In this realm of white, we find our place,
Embracing the chill, a warm-hearted grace.

## The Heart Beneath the Frost

Underneath the snow, life silently thrives,
Roots hold firm, where the earth derives.
Warmth lingers deep, beneath icy crust,
Life's gentle pulse, a promise of trust.

Through the chill, green whispers awake,
The heart beneath begins to break.
Resilience blooms from the bitter cold,
A story of patience, quietly told.

Crystal branches sway with grace,
Winter's spell, a fleeting embrace.
Hope stirs softly in every chill,
Reminders of warmth, the soul to fill.

When spring arrives, the thaw will be sweet,
Life renews where frost and warmth meet.
The heart beats on, despite winter's cost,
In every layer, not a moment lost.

## Nature's Shimmering Blanket

A quilt of white drapes the earth,
Softly wrapped, it sings of mirth.
Each flake unique, a frosty sight,
Nature's beauty, pure and bright.

Under stars, the landscape glows,
Silent whispers in powdery snows.
Trees bow down with a heavy crown,
Embracing night in barely a frown.

Morning sun paints a sparkling hue,
Melting the chill, revealing new.
Footprints wander on paths so still,
Discovering magic, the heart they fill.

In every corner, wonder lies,
Nature's art, beneath open skies.
A shimmering blanket, soft and wide,
Where peace and beauty forever abide.

## Softly Floating Wishes

In the air, dreams take flight,
Snowflakes twirl in the pale moonlight.
Each one carries a whispered hope,
Softly drifting, a magical scope.

On winter's breath, wishes ascend,
Carried forth, on the chill they depend.
Gently they land on the sleeping ground,
In this quiet, their dreams surround.

Hearts entwined, as the night deepens,
Embracing visions, the soul stiffens.
With every flurry, a promise takes wing,
Softly floating, the joy they bring.

As dawn breaks, the wishes unfold,
Stories together, perfected and bold.
In winter's embrace, we find our way,
Softly floating, come what may.

## Hushed Adventures in Cold

The snowflakes dance, so light and free,
Footsteps crunch in quiet glee.
Trees wear coats of purest white,
In the hush of soft twilight.

Whispers echo through the frost,
In this land where heat is lost.
Every breath hangs in the air,
A frozen world, serene, and rare.

Pathways lead to dreams untold,
In the wonders, brave and bold.
Adventures hide in icy trails,
Where magic glows, and silence sails.

With every turn, a new surprise,
In this realm where beauty lies.
Hushed adventures, secrets kept,
In this world where stillness wept.

## Meadows of Silence

In meadows wide, the stillness grows,
Where softest winds and silence flows.
Grasses bend in gentle sway,
A tranquil scene, by light of day.

Blossoms hide beneath cool shade,
Nature’s peace, a sweet cascade.
Butterflies drift through the air,
Whispers of joy linger there.

The brook hums low a soothing tune,
While shadows play 'neath the bright moon.
In these fields, hearts find their rest,
Meadows of silence, nature’s best.

Moments pause as time stands still,
In the quiet, we can heal.
Embrace the peace where dreams align,
In meadows rich with love divine.

## Winter's Playful Whisper

Winter drapes the world in white,
As day gives way to cozy night.
A playful whisper in the air,
Brings laughter forth without a care.

Children spin in frosty glow,
Creating castles in the snow.
Snowball fights and sleds that glide,
In winter's arms, we find our pride.

The hearth burns bright, a warm embrace,
While frosty winds begin to race.
Hot cocoa warms the chilly hands,
As we share dreams and make new plans.

Magic dances in the night,
As stars twinkle with soft light.
Winter's whisper, crisp and clear,
Invites our hearts to hold it near.

## The Stillness of Frigid Air

The world holds breath in frigid air,
Each moment wrapped in silence fair.
A crystal hush lies deep and wide,
Where secrets of the heart abide.

Frosted branches, artful sway,
Kindred spirits at the break of day.
Echoes of nature, sweet and low,
In the stillness, magic flows.

Underneath the vast blue skies,
Winter's blanket softly lies.
In the quiet, dreams take flight,
Guided by the stars at night.

Awakened souls find solace here,
With every breath, the world is clear.
In this stillness, we find our place,
Embraced by winter's calming grace.

Milton Keynes UK
Ingram Content Group UK Ltd.
UKHW021241191124
451300UK00007B/171

9 789916 944523